NOTES

ON

Printing Papers Suitable for Maps

AND ON

Whatman's Drawing Paper

Printed by Order of the Surveyor-General of India

CALCUTTA
SUPERINTENDENT GOVERNMENT PRINTING, INDIA
1911

Notes on Printing Papers Suitable for Maps.

In letter No. 477, dated 3rd February 1910, from the Surveyor-General of India to the Government of India in the Revenue and Agriculture Department, it was requested that, in the event of my being ordered to visit the offices of the Ordnance Survey and of Messrs. Bartholomew & W. & A. K. Johnston in connection with rubber offset printing, I should also report on the paper found most suitable for printing maps.

1. General.

None of the papers that I saw in use appear quite to meet all requirements for map printing as to strength, printing qualities and appearance.

At Southampton the topographical maps are mostly printed on Cowan's rag litho paper (the same paper as is used by the Survey of India). All issues for military purposes are, I believe, mounted on nainsuk cloth. Rag litho paper which has first-class printing qualities is weak, stands crumpling and folding badly, and has no resistance to water.

2. Papers in use for map printing.

Messrs. Bartholomew and W. & A. K. Johnston use several varieties of paper, among them Messrs. Cowan's papers but none that I saw appeared to combine printing qualities and appearance with lightness and strength in any very marked degree.

At the War Office the following descriptions of papers are used :—

For ordinary maps (light). A paper inferior in surface and appearance to Messrs. Cowan's rag litho, but apparently a little stronger than that paper.

For ordinary maps. A heavier and harder paper, fairly strong, but it does not stand folding or crumpling well.

For military purposes in the field :—

A light paper mounted on cloth. This gives a very strong material, but it does not stand folding or crumpling very well, and is heavy and bulky.

B

3. Necessity for further investigation.

It is not, however, possible for any one but an expert to judge papers accurately without chemical and instrumental tests. With the aid of testing equipment it would probably be possible to give specifications for a specially made paper * which should be superior for map printing purposes to any of the papers now generally in use, and more economical than the Insetsukioku Japanese paper which is now being supplied to the Survey of India.

So far as I can judge, Japanese Insetsukioku paper combines printing qualities with strength and resistance to water far better than any of the papers I have seen in use; it has, however, the serious defect of being expensive, and the minor defect of not being quite white in colour.

4 Arrangement of these notes.

In the following notes I have compiled the information obtained from books and from visits to Messrs. Cowan's and Messrs. Balston's paper mills under the heads of the special characteristics which I believe to be desirable in papers used for Indian maps.

I have also described the various tests which are necessary for the practical investigation of the subject.

5. Characteristics that are required in map papers.

To be suitable for maps, paper should possess the following characteristics :—

(1) It must be sufficiently smooth and absorbent, without being too absorbent, in order to take up the ink from fine lines and dots on the plate. The introduction of rubber offset printing would render smoothness unnecessary.

(2) It must be tough to resist :—

breaking under tensile strain, and bursting;

tearing;

crumpling and folding.

(3) It should stand being wet.

(4) It should be a pure white colour and opaque. Much glaze is considered objectionable.

(5) It should retain the above qualities with age.

---

* NOTE.—Paper makers can make any special paper, provided 1 ton is ordered.

(6) It should vary in dimensions as little as possible with atmospheric humidity.

(7) It should be light in weight. For military purposes large numbers of sheets may have to be carried in the field.

5. Characteristics that are required in map papers —contd.

Until it is sized, paper is too absorbent for printing. The size fills up the pores of the paper thus preventing the ink spreading by capillary attraction.

6. Sizing.

Generally speaking the best and most expensive papers are "gelatine," that is, "animal" sized.

All hand-made papers and those machine-made papers that are ' loft ' dried, i.e., dried slowly, are gelatine sized.

Ordinary papers are resin sized, but some papers are both resin sized and gelatine sized. A gelatine sized paper presents an impenetrable surface to printing, and when printed, the ink dries slowly and is liable to smudge. Gelatine sized papers are sometimes liable to putrify if the gelatine is not pure.

The best printing papers are stated to be those that are practically unsized except with starch.

Though quantitative analysis of paper requires some special chemical knowledge the following tests can be made by any one :—

(a) For presence of ' size '; mark the paper with ink, the less the ink spreads the greater the degree of sizing.

Papers of equal thickness may be compared as to sizing thus :—

Drop simultaneously one drop of aniline blue dissolved in methylated spirits on the papers, and time the appearance of the blue on the back of each.

(b) For "animal" or "gelatine" size :—

Tear a sample into shreds and place in a test tube. Cover with water and boil for a few minutes. Pour off the clear liquid, add a drop of tannic acid, gelatine is precipitated if present.

6. Sizing—
conta.

(c) For starch :—

Dip a corner of the paper into iodide of potassium, treat with a drop or two of chlorine water, starch is indicated by a blue colouration.

(d) If neither gelatine nor starch be present, ' resin ' may be inferred ; but as some papers are both gelatine and resin sized, if gelatine is present, to test for resin :—get rid of all traces of gelatine by boiling in clear water, drain off the shreds, cover them with spirits-of-wine, shake and then pass the clear liquid through filter paper into a clean test tube, and add a few drops of alum water. Resin, if present, is precipitated in a thin white powder.

7. Strength.

Strength depends on the length and quality of the fibre and its being well interlaced or woven. The best fibres used in England are linen and cotton. They may be distinguished under the microscope ; as the former has a jointed appearance like bamboo and the latter is flat. Plates showing the appearance of the different fibres under the microscope are given in R. W. Sindall's "Paper Technicology" (Griffen & Co., London). The interlacing of the fibres is effected by a transverse shake communicated to the liquid ' stuff,' by the machine in machine-made papers, or by the moulder in hand-made papers. For long it was claimed that the latter was the more effective, and that hand-made papers are necessarily stronger than machine-made papers. There was formerly reason for this, because, while the moulds used for hand-made paper were "laid," that is consisted of parallel wires, machine-made papers were moulded on woven wire, and this allowed the use of a shorter fibre than could be used in laid moulds. Modern tests have however shown, that given equal "stock" and weight, machine-made and hand-made papers are about equally strong if the former is tested in its weaker direction, but, that if it be tested in its "machine direction," it is 20% to 25% stronger than hand-made paper. Hand-made papers are still usually made only of the best stock, carefully and slowly mixed, and are loft dried, but machine-made papers can be, and often are, their equals in these respects.

There are several instruments designed to test the strength of paper : they measure either the tensile strain under which the paper breaks, or the bursting strain under which it is penetrated by a small cylinder.

Tensile strain testers also record the temporary expansion of the paper at breaking point. Bursting strain instruments have the advantage that they do not require the very accurate adjustment of carefully cut strips, free from notches, and aligned exactly between clamps.

The instrument used at the India Office Store Department, at the Ordnance Survey Office, and by many paper makers, is a tensile strain balance by E. Leunig, London. Neither the experts at the India Office nor the paper makers I consulted consider this mode of testing satisfactory, and one of the former told me that in some cases the results are very misleading.

I saw the following results obtained on a Leunig paper tester at the India Office :—

Paper.	Breaking strain in lbs. in stronger direction.
Hollingworth (131 lbs.)	24
Cowan's rag litho 67 lbs. . . .	14
Insetsukioku G. 1. 29 lbs. . . .	18·5
,, ,, ,, 2. 43 lbs. . . .	20
,, ,, ,, 3. 61 lbs. . . .	35

Messrs. Cowan are now using an American " bursting " strain tester, the 'Mullen' paper tester, (sold by the Parson's Trading Company, 171, Queen Victoria Street, E. C., price £15-15-0). They consider the results obtained from this instrument more useful as a guide to the strength of paper, than those obtained from " tensile " strain instruments. The same instrument is also used in the Ordnance Survey.

Mr. Gardner of Messrs. Cowan & Co., kindly tested the following papers for me in a 'Mullen' paper tester.

Paper.	Bursting strain in lbs. per sq. inch.
Insetsukioku G. 1. 28lbs. (17½″ × 22½″) .	79·1
Cowan's 'Wood' papers, No. 1-886 .	35·3

The wood paper was selected for testing because it bears a great resemblance to the Insetsukioku paper, which Mr. Gardner believed to be made from mulberry fibre.

Other testing machines are :—the Schoppenhaner, used by the German Government ; Marshall's, much used in England ; Carrington's used for brown paper by the Stationery Office ; Southworths, and Woolly's. I did not see any of these instruments.

Strength to stand crumpling and folding may be tested thus :—Cut a 6″ square and fold as shewn in the diagram, again fold in the same creases, but in the reverse direction. After every ten foldings the appearance of the centre of the sheet should be noted, and after 120 foldings, strips cut as shewn should be tested in a tensile strain machine.

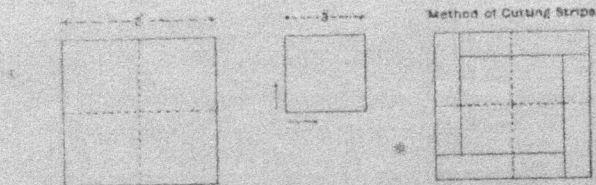

Arrows show direction in which the folds should be pressed.

Experts judge resistance to folding, by folding and refolding in the reversed direction, the corner of a sheet, and judging the strain required to pull off the corner with a direct pull.

Breaking in folding does not necessarily indicate weak fibre, it may be due to :—

(i) too high a temperature at the drying cylinders ;

(ii) excess of loading material ;

(iii) over boiling ;

(iv) over bleaching ;

(v) too much antichlor.

This quality does not seem to be much in demand, it is however desirable for map papers. I heard of no special tests, but when at Calcutta I tested several makes of paper by crumpling them up and soaking in water for 2 minutes.

Insetsukioku paper stood this test very well. Hollingworth (131 ℔ D. E.) stood it fairly well, and rag litho paper fell to pieces during the test.

Surface does not vary with quality. Any degree of smoothness can be obtained by calendering, *i.e.*, passing the paper between a series of hard rollers. Some manufacturers consider that plate pressing gives a superior surface than calendering, and it has the advantage that it does not reduce the thickness of the paper. It is however a slow and expensive process as each sheet has to be placed between zinc plates and the pile pressed, and then unpiled, repiled, and repressed. Even an expert cannot always say, except by the plate marks, whether a sheet of paper has been plate pressed or calendered. Hot pressing, a still more expensive process, is now obsolete.

The highest polishing is procured by burnishing. An entire absence of glaze or ' dead finish ' is necessary if the water-mark must be retained ; bank-note paper is dead finished.

Even an inferior or a naturally brown material may be severely bleached to produce a good white bright colour, but this weakens the paper, and the colour produced by it is not permanent. It may be necessary to sacrifice appearance to some extent to strength. This is probably the case with Japanese Insetsukioku paper. For map purposes a slightly brown colour is immaterial in comparison with strength.

10. Permanence.

There is little doubt that much of the cheaper paper now in use, made from wood and inferior pulps, will deteriorate with age. For permanence, in addition to being of a good fibre, it is necessary that the paper should be free from acid, from bleaching chemicals and from 'loading' or mineral matter.

Good paper when digested in hot water, should yield a liquid neutral to test paper. To test for mineral matter :—Weigh a small sample, tear it into shreds, burn it in a platinum crucible heated to redness and weigh the residual ash. As there is some mineral matter in the original materials from which paper is made, few, if any, papers are absolutely free from it, and papers that yield 1% or less of ash, may be considered as free from loading.

Loading when used merely to improve the surface and add to its whiteness is not necessarily deleterious, 5% of loading should be sufficient for this. Loading should not be used to give body or substance to a paper.

11. Expansion with humidity.

There does not seem to be any standard test for this; paper-makers test for it roughly by measuring paper before and after damping. To render the results useful for reference, the paper should be thoroughly dried and then tested at known degrees of humidity after it has absorbed a known proportion of water.

Expansion is always least in the machine direction and this should be borne in mind in printing.

To ascertain the machine direction, float a circular disc of the paper on water keeping the upper surface unwet, when removed from the water the disc will roll up into a cylinder, the axis of which is parallel to the machine direction. Another method is to cut strips at right angles to each other and parallel to the edges of the sheet, the weaker strip will be the less stiff and will fall away from the stronger if both are held up from their lower ends.

12. To distinguish machine-made from hand-made paper.

(i) Machine-made paper is stronger in one direction than the other, it tears more easily and with a smoother edge in the machine direction. Hand-made paper tears equally easily and with an equally fibrous edge in any direction.

(*ii*) Hand-made papers have 'deckle' edges, *i.e.*, rough unfinished edges.

(*iii*) A wire cloth mark is always present in machine-made 'laid' papers.

(*iv*) In wove papers, the water-mark is more distinct in machine-made, than in hand-made papers. The water-mark can generally be seen when looking along the surface of a machine-made paper.

(*v*) The mesh in wove hand-made papers is generally wide (40 to 60 to the inch). In machine-made papers it runs up to 80 to one inch.

Paper should always be printed on its right side. It is not always easy to distinguish the right side, the following indications are of assistance :—

(*a*) On opening a ream of flat paper the right side is found uppermost.

(*b*, When paper is folded into quires the right side is outside.

(*c*) The lettering of water-marks reads from the right side. Folded office papers are an exception, as the water-mark is read on the 1st and 3rd page.

(*d*) The wire cloth mark is on the wrong side in machine-made papers.

(*e*) Either side may be the rougher.

At Southampton the samples supplied with tenders for paper are tested annually. Both a Leunig and a Muller testing machine are used, the fibre is examined under a microscope and the sizing and loading and acidity are tested for.

At the India Office Stores Department there is equipment for testing, and a certain proportion of papers are tested, the better papers such as Cowan's rag letters are not as a rule tested.

Notes on Drawing Paper, made during a visit to Messrs. Balston's Mills, where the Whatman's Drawing Papers are made.

Before issue the papers are tested to see how they stand erasure, and it is found that they improve in this respect with seasoning. Mr. Balston believes this is because the gelatine size requires time and humidity to thoroughly permeate the paper. Almost all the Whatman paper is seasoned for some months in the mills before issue.

The surface of ordinary drawing paper is not smooth enough for map drawing; practically any degree of smoothness and roughness can be obtained, if specially ordered.

Messrs. Balston make a special very heavy 300 ℔. Imperial paper; if given a smoother surface it should prove useful for field sections. This weight of paper is not made larger than Imperial size, as it would be too heavy to handle during manufacture.

Drawing papers can be supplied in other than the standard sizes; this is however expensive and means the provision of special moulds. Sizes less than the standard sizes by about an inch in each dimension can however be provided, at no extra cost, by temporarily adding strips of wood or metal within the edges of the moulds.

The white of the Whatman papers inclines to a yellow tint; paper with a slightly blue tinge could be made at a slightly greater cost.

I am indebted to Mr. R. W. Sindall's "Paper Technicology" for much of the information contained in these notes, and also to the gentlemen named below for courteous permission to visit their offices or mills and for kindly showing me the different processes of paper manufacture and testing :—

The Director General, Ordnance Survey.

The Director, Stores Department, the India Office.

Messrs. Cowan & Sons, Valleyfield, Pennycuik.

Messrs. Alexander Cowan & Co., Musselborough.

Messrs. Balston, Maidstone.

W. M. COLDSTREAM, *Major, R.E.,*
Offg. Superintendent of Map Publication.

CALCUTTA
SUPERINTENDENT GOVERNMENT PRINTING, INDIA
8, HASTINGS STREET

www.ingramcontent.com/pod-product-compliance
Lightning Source LLC
Chambersburg PA
CBHW081455070426
42452CB00042B/2746